Part E
Changes in Transport

Good transport and communications are aspects of our life that we take for granted. In 1700 the transport system in Britain was probably worse than it had been in Roman times! If it had stayed that way, none of the great changes described in this book could have happened. An improved transport system was a vital part of the Industrial Revolution.

13 Travel by road

In 1700 there were only two ways of travelling in Britain. Anyone carrying heavy goods would, as far as possible, use the rivers and the sea. But many places were too far from either.

The only alternative was roads. In 1700 the law said that every person should give up six days each year to keep local roads in good repair.

Barges on the River Medway, Kent.

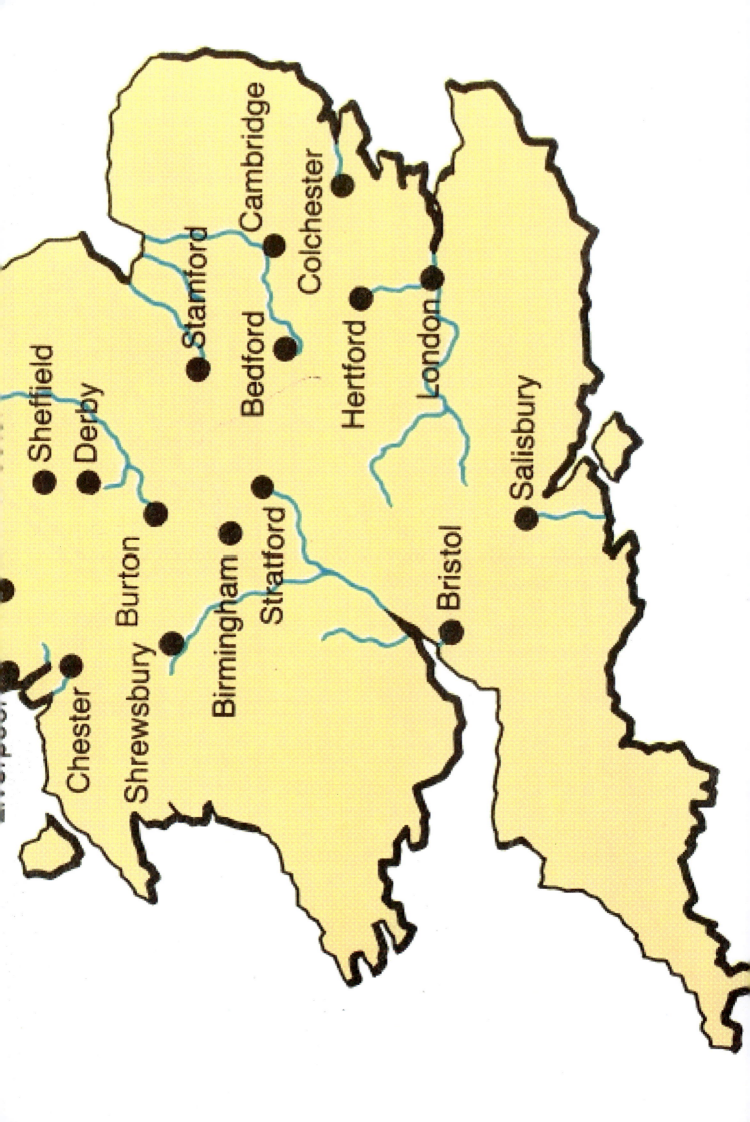

page 66

Newcastle

York

Leeds

Manchester

Liverpool

Navigable rivers in Britain in 1700.

page 67

Arthur Young's description of a road in 1771 shows how badly the system worked in part of Lancashire:

Let me warn all travellers to avoid this damned road as they would the devil. For a thousand to one, they will break their limbs by overthrowing or breaking down. They will meet with ruts which I actually measured four feet deep and floating with mud after a wet I summer. The only mending the road gets is the tumbling in of some loose stones.

67 c. 1

Here the writer Daniel Defoe describes the state of roads in the Midlands, and what was done about it:

There is very great trade between the Midland counties and the City of London. The roads had been plowed very deep, and in some districts it is difficult to get materials for repair. It is so bad that these things have been brought before Parliament.

As a consequence, turnpikes or toll bars have been set up on the great roads of England. At the turnpikes all carriages, droves of cattle, and travellers on horseback are obliged to pay a toll. Several of the turnpikes have been set up, and it is incredible what effect it has had. Even the cost of carrying goods has fallen - in some places 6d. per cwt. - with greater safety and ease of travelling, and the speeding up of the post.

Questions

1 Look at the map. Identify three areas of England or Wales that are important for industry today, but which could not benefit from the use of rivers for transport in 1700.

2 Why do you think the old roads, as described by Young and Defoe, had become so bad?

3 Why was the old system of road repair unlikely to work?

4 Complete the diagram, which explains how turnpike roads worked.

5 What were the benefits of turnpikes, according to Defoe?

67 c. 3

poor surface	solid bridge
good drainage	turnpike
direct route	turnpike road
good surface	ruts and pools
old road	turnpike cottage
roads splaying across nearby fields	

67 c. 4

page 68

The idea of turnpike roads caught on. By 1750 there were 150 turnpike trusts, controlling 3400 miles of road. Fifty years later, 20 000 miles were controlled by turnpike trusts.

Engineers were appointed to build new roads. The two most famous road-builders were Thomas Telford and John McAdam. These diagrams show how they built their roads.

THOMAS TELFORD'S ROADS

Telford built his roads with gentle gradients on straight lines. These were marvellous roads such as the London-Holyhead road but were very expensive - only the government could afford to build them.

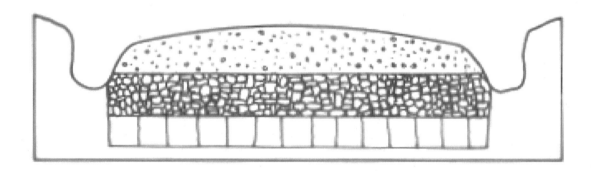

- gravel surface
- layers of stones packed firmly on top
- cambered surface
- ditch at side for drainage
- solid foundation of blocks of stone

JOHN McADAM'S ROADS

McAdam's roads were quick and cheap to build, and were very popular with turnpike trusts.

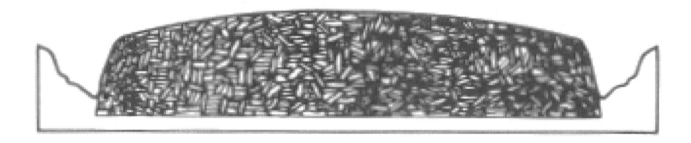

- chippings packed tightly together
- road above level of surrounding land cambered surface ditch for drainage

Questions

1. Copy and label the diagrams.
2. In what way was each method better than the other?

Roads do not seem as spectacular to us as do the railways, but here are some examples of the engineering marvels of the road system.

The Clifton Suspension Bridge, Bristol.

The Menai Bridge, Gwynedd.

Travel on the new roads

People wanting to travel from London to York in 1706 would have seen posters like this:

YORK Four Days Stage-Coach.

Begins on Friday the 12th of April 1706.

ALL that are desirous to pass from *London* to *York*, or from *York* to *London*, or any other Place on that Road; Let them Repair to the *Black Swan* in *Holbourn* in *London*, and to the *Black Swan* in *Coney-street* in *York*.

At both which Places, they may be received in a Stage Coach every *Monday*, *Wednesday* and *Friday*, which performs the whole Journey in Four Days, (*if God permits.*) And sets forth at Five in the Morning.

And returns from *York* to *Stamford* in two days, and from *Stamford* by *Huntington* to *London* in two days more. And the like Stages on their return.

Allowing each Passenger 14*l*, weight, and all above 3*d*. a Pound.

Performed By { Benjamin Kingman, Henry Harrison, Walter Baynes,

Also this gives Notice that Newcastle Stage Coach, sets out from York, every Monday, and Friday, and from Newcastle every Monday, and Friday.

Rec͟d in pt. 05-00. of Mr. Bodingfold for 5 p͟ld
for Monday the 3 of June 1706

69 c. 2

A painting of the Royal Mail coaches.

All along the way these coaches used to stop at roadside inns for refreshment and to change horses. Even so, it must have been a relief to get to the journey's end. As can be seen from this newspaper article of 1807, road transport steadily improved.

69 c. 3

In the year 1770 there was only one coach to London, and one to Liverpool, which went from or came into Manchester, and they set out only twice a week. There are now 27 distinct coaches which run from Manchester, of which 18 set out every day.

In the year 1754 a 'flying coach' was advertised and it promised the following: 'However incredible it might appear it will actually arrive in London in four days and a half after leaving Manchester'. The distance is 185 'Miles and the journey is now performed by mail-coaches in about thirty hours, and on some occasions it has been travelled in twenty hours.

The Weekly Dispatch,

6 September 1807

page 70

This improvement can partly be explained by better roads. However, the following account shows how the coaches themselves were built for greater speed.

The New Mail Coach has travelled with a speed that is really astonishing, having seldom taken longer than thirteen hours in going to or returning from London. It is made very light, carries four passengers and runs with a pair of horses, which exchange every six or eight miles; and as the mail bags at the different offices are prepared before its arrival, there is never any delay. The guard rides with the coachman on the box, and the mail is deposited in the boot. By this means the inhabitants of Gloucester and Bristol have the London letters a day earlier than usual.

The Gloucester journal, 16 August 1784

However, there were limits to the speed at which the poor horses could go:

> By 1830, the coaching system was perfect. The horses were changed in a few brief seconds; the coachmen were fined heavily if they arrived late; horses were bred especially for coaching, and in some cases were urged so much that they fell with excitement and died of a broken blood vessel or a broken heart.

Francis, 1851

70 c. 2

Questions

1   Look at the three routes marked on the map. On each one write the time of the journey before improvement, and the time after improvement.

2   List all the ways you can find in which stage-coach travel was made quicker.

Key

Approximate travelling time, from London:

——	distance between lines = 1 day's travel before 1750
··············	distance between lines = 1 day's travel after 1820

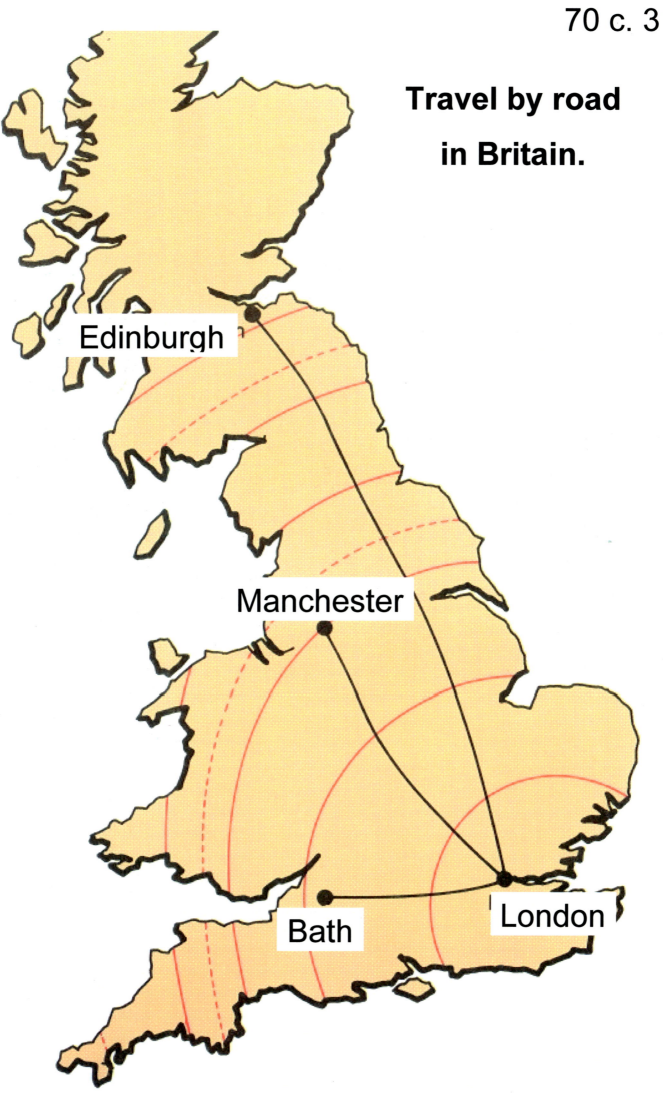

70 c. 4

Problems of road travel

So far we have been looking at **improvements** in roads. Some roads, however, were not improved for many years, or not at all. This account shows what could go wrong when a turnpike trust paid someone else to do the work. This was called 'farming' the work.

So there were still bad roads. And even on the good ones, travel could be dangerous.

70 c. 5

The trustees, when once a road is farmed, have nothing to do but meet once a year to eat venison and pay the farmer his salary. The farmer has nothing to do, but to do as little work, and pocket as much money, as he possibly can; he has other fish to fry, other matters to mind, than road-mending. The roads become overgrown, and rainwater and narrow-wheeled waggons ruin the surface. At length, the complaints of travellers and the menace of court proceedings, rouse the trustees. A meeting is called for, the farmer is sent for and reprimanded, and a few loads of gravel are thrown into the mud to keep the road passable.

Digests of the General Highway and the Turnpike Laws, by John Scott, 1778

page 71

Here, a visitor to England in 1782 describes what it was like to travel on top of the coach:

I had to sit at the corner of the coach, with nothing to hold but a little handle. I sat nearest the wheel, and when we set off, I fancied I saw certain death awaiting me. The machine rolled over the stones through the town and every moment we seemed to fly into the air.

This was not the only danger. Read these two stories:

Joseph had not gone above two miles ... when he was met by two fellows in a narrow lane, and ordered to stand and deliver. He readily gave them all the money he had, which was somewhat less than two pounds. He asked them to return a few shillings to finish his journey.

One of the ruffians answered with an oath, 'Yes, we'll give you something soon'; but first 'Strip', cried the other, 'or I'll blow your brains to the devil!' Joseph said he hoped they would not take his clothes, which were not worth much, but that the night was cold. 'You are cold, are you, rascal?', said one of the robbers: 'I'll warm you up', and damning his eyes snapped a pistol at his head, while the other aimed a blow at him with his stick. Joseph caught the cudgel and felled the robber, but at the same moment was hit on the head from behind with the butt end of a pistol, which felled him to the ground and knocked him out.

71 c. 2

On Thursday morning at 3 o'clock a single highwayman attempted to rob the Stamford Fly. He ordered the coachman to stop, but the guard, who travels with the coach, told him to keep off, or he would shoot him. When the highwayman persisted, the guard fired a blunderbuss and lodged two slugs in his forehead. He was put in the basket of the coach, where he lived but a few minutes. Before his death he confessed that he had robbed the Peterborough stage a fortnight before. He had no firearms about him, but made use of a candle instead of a pistol.

Norwich Mercury, 17 September 1774

The Bath-London mail coach. The man in the post office hands over the mailbags as the coach passes without stopping.

Activity

Defoe, Young and others wrote down their experiences travelling round the country. Use all of the information above to write an account of a journey. Remember that the traveller will have met different road conditions, and that people will have had different feelings about their experiences on the road.

14 Canals

Barton Bridge: an aqueduct over the River Irwell.

We have seen that passenger travel by road improved in many ways. Transport of goods, however, did not. A new system of transport was needed for heavy goods.

72 c. 1

A tunnel entrance on the Bridgewater canal.

72 c. 2

The Duke of Bridgewater, who owned coal mines at Worsley in Lancashire, needed a better way to get his coal to Manchester. He knew about canals in Europe, and decided to have one built for himself. His canal was so spectacular that people came from far away to see it. Here is a description, starting from the Barton aqueduct:

72 c. 3

At Barton bridge he has built a canal in the air; for it is as high as the tops of the trees. While I was looking at it with a mixture of wonder and delight, four barges passed me in about three minutes. Two were chained together, and pulled by two horses who pulled them from the towpath across the aqueduct. I confess, I was scared to walk across and look down to the River Irwell beneath.

From Barton I steered towards the mines. In places the canal passed over roads and bogs. The canal begins at the foot of some hills, where the Duke's coals are cut. The canal is cut through the rocks into this hill, where the light never enters. Large boats are hauled into the mine, are filled with coals, and brought out by an easy current.

Annual Register, 1763

page 73

Questions

1 What part of the Duke of Bridgewater's canal seems most to have impressed the writer?

2 Find three things about this canal that made it particularly efficient.

3 Which do you find more useful as evidence of what the canal was like: the description of the canal, or the pictures? Explain your answer carefully.

73 c. 1

The problems of building canals

Two particular problems faced canal builders. The first was to keep a high level of water in the canals. The second was to find a way of building canals where the ground sloped.

The first problem was solved by diverting water from rivers into the source of the canal. To stop the water seeping out again, the canal bed had to be made watertight. If a material like stone was used on the canal bed, it made the canal very expensive to build. However, a much cheaper lining was found - clay which had been 'puddled' to make it watertight.

The second problem, that of building canals on sloping ground, was much more difficult. Study each of these examples of how the problem was solved (A-E).

73 c. 1

The Llangollen canal and the Pont Cysyllte aqueduct.

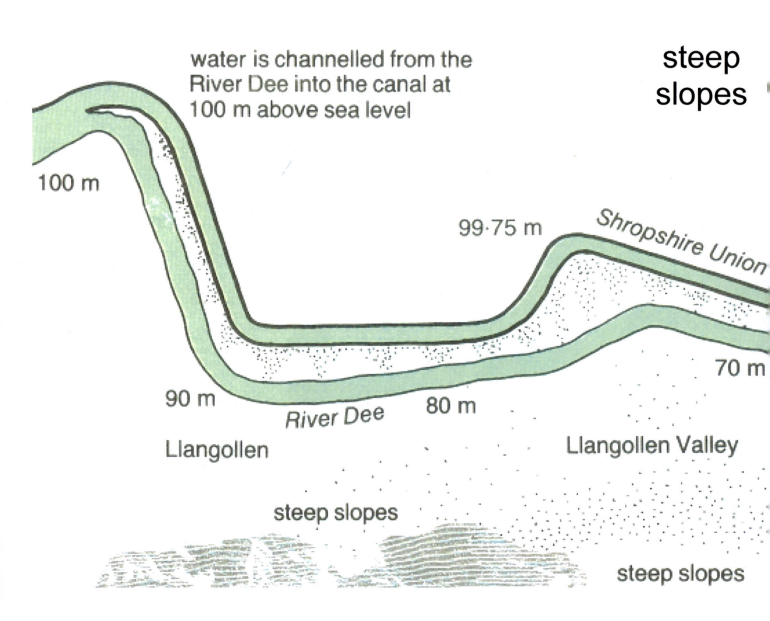

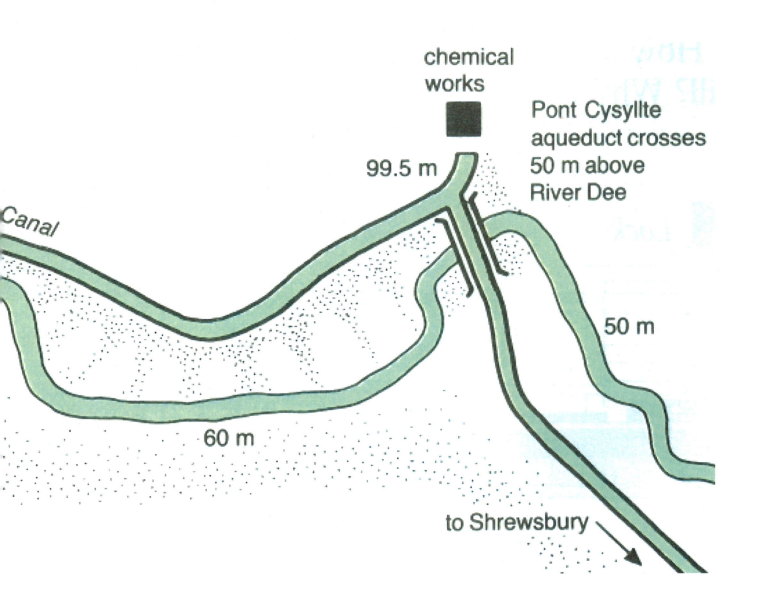

Question

This canal was built by Thomas Telford.

The canal is in a sloping valley, and crosses a river. How did Telford solve each of these problems?

B The Harecastle tunnels.

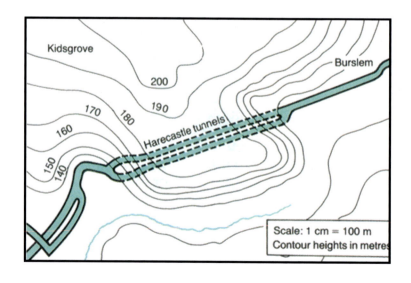

74 c. 1

Burslem

Kidsgrove

Harecastle tunnels

200

190

180

170

160

150

140

Scale:

Contour heights in metres

74 c. 2

Questions

1 Hills blocked the route of this canal.

How was this problem solved?

2 How long is the tunnel?

How high is the hill?

Why couldn't the canal go round the hill?

3 Look carefully at the picture.

Find two differences between the first

tunnel (1777) and the second (1827).

74 c. 3

ACTIVITY

Draw your own version of the lock system and label your diagram using the following descriptions:

- Barge enters lock at low level.

- Lower gate is closed and upper sluice opens.

- Water level in lower lock is raised to height of upper level.

- Upper gate is opened and barge can be towed out.

C Locks

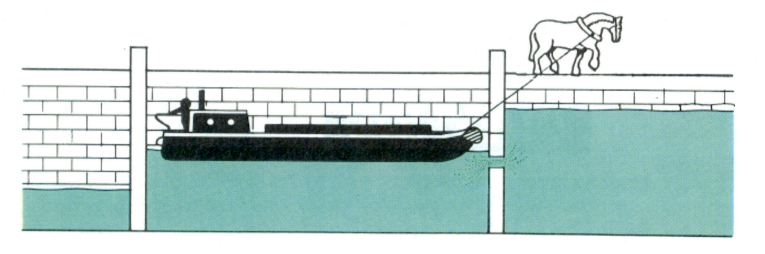

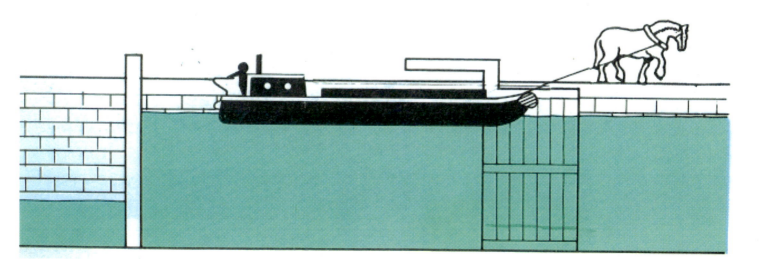

page 75

D An inclined plane.

The cradles are pulled up the incline, then over the lip into the upper canal.

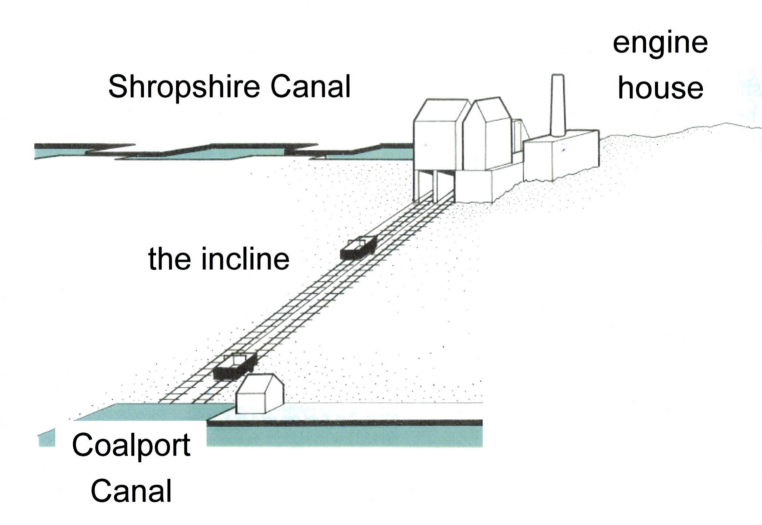

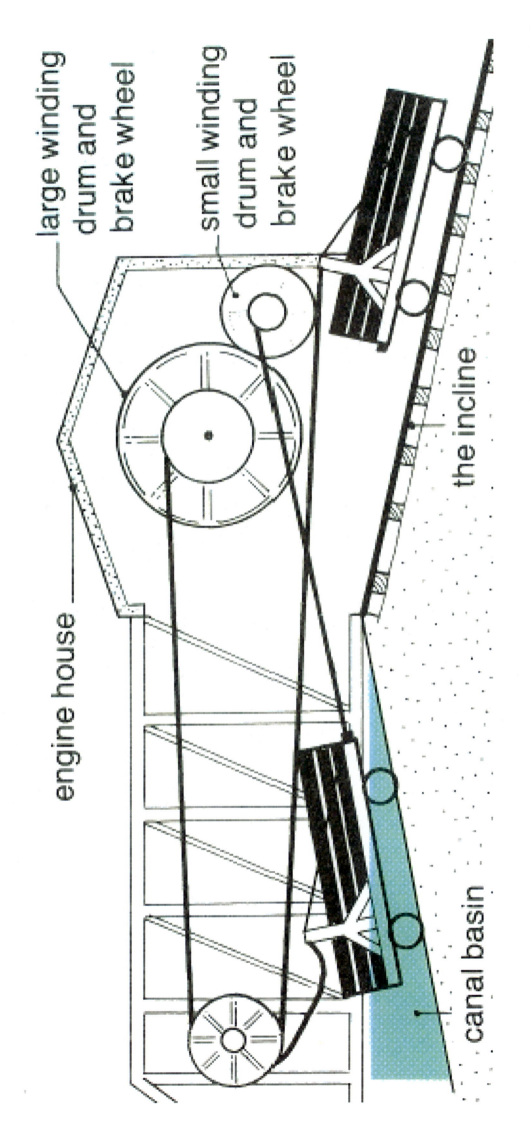

ACTIVITIES

1 The inclined plane could work before the development of steam power. Use the diagram to show how.

2 Why do you think the Anderton lift has been described as 'a wonder of the Industrial Revolution'? Think about its appearance as well as the way it works.

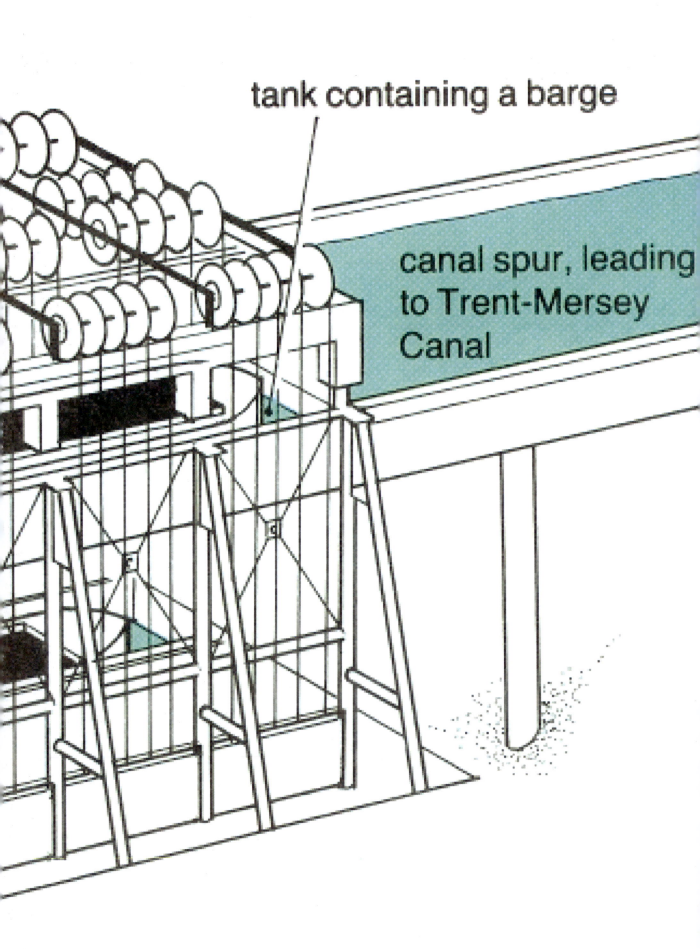

page 75 **E   The Anderton lift.**

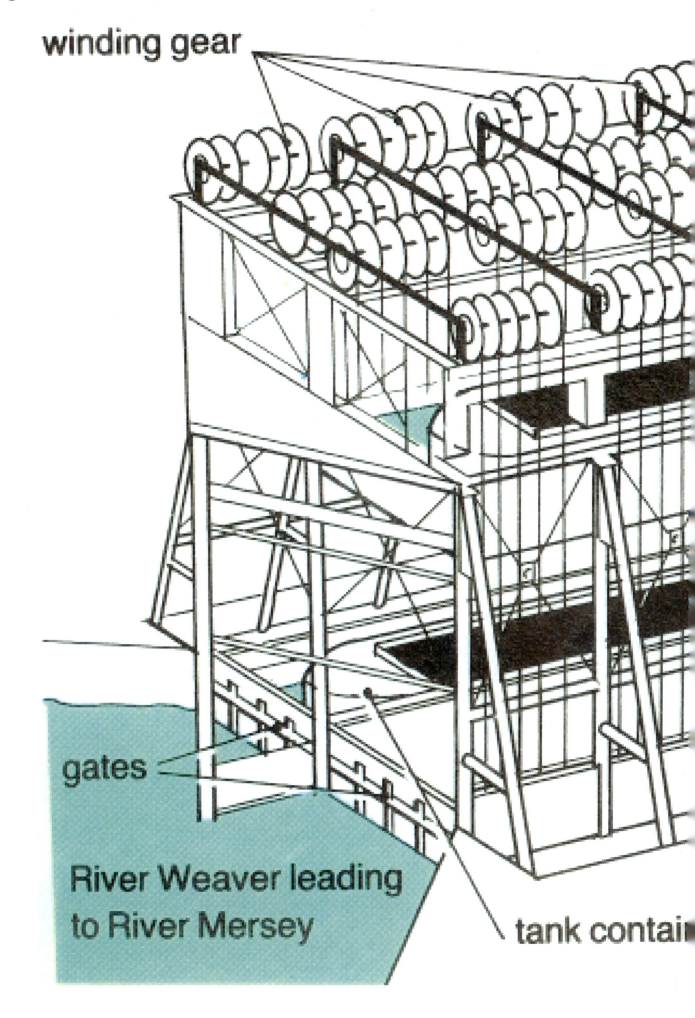

E The Anderton lift.

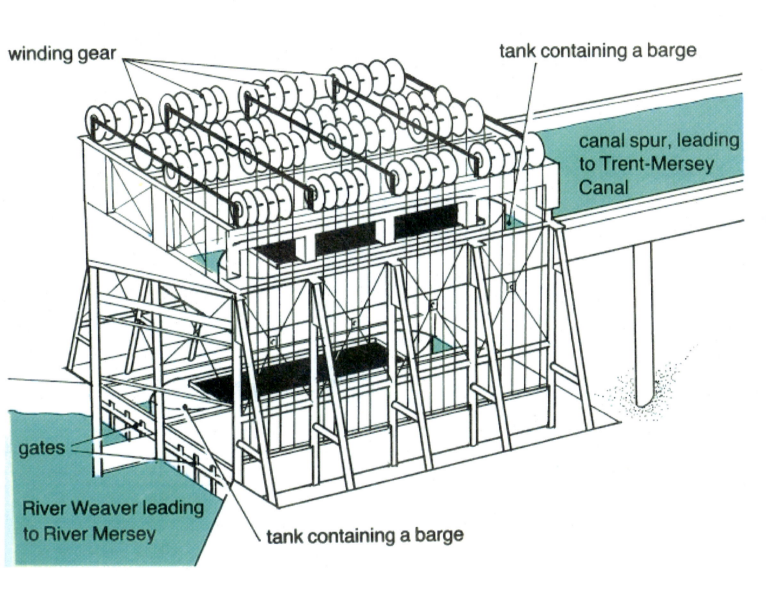

Who gained from the canals?

The Bridgewater canal showed that heavy and bulky goods could be carried cheaply. Soon afterwards other people copied the idea and a network of canals was built. You can see this on the map.

At first the people who built canals were those who needed them to transport a particular type of goods. We have seen, for example, that the Duke of Bridgewater wanted to get coal from Worsley to Manchester. Look at the map and you will see why Josiah Wedgwood wanted a canal from his potteries in Staffordshire to the River Mersey. Later, however, people realised that canals could be built to any important city, and from one side of the country to the other.

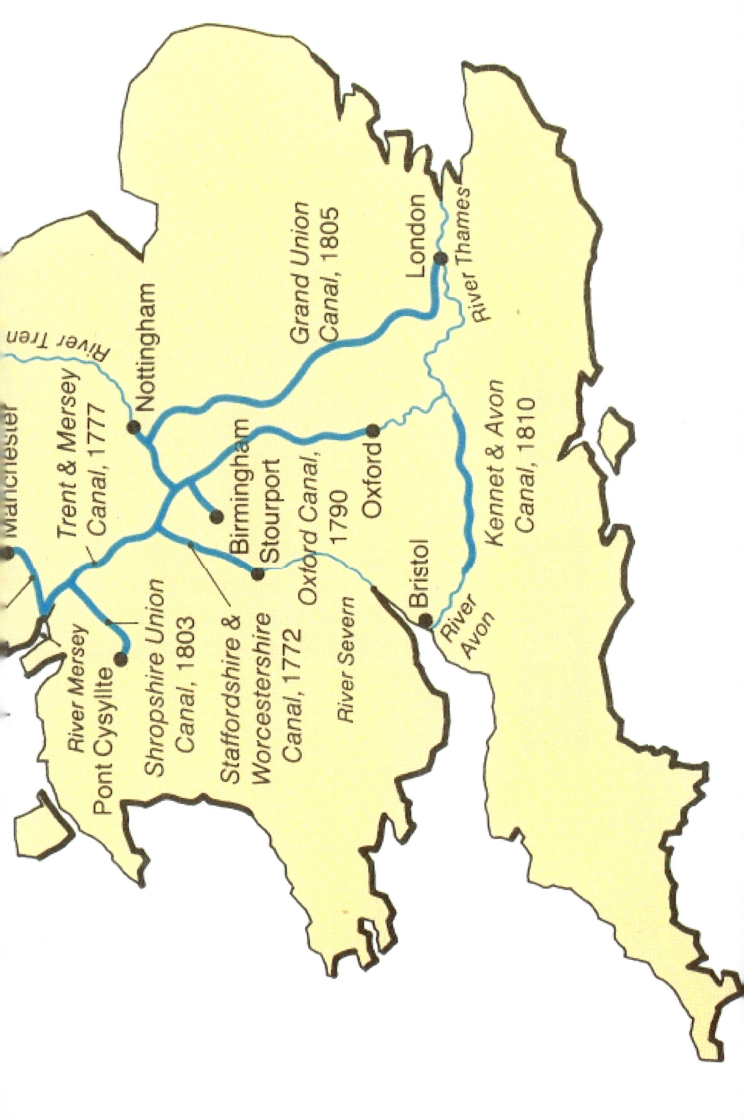

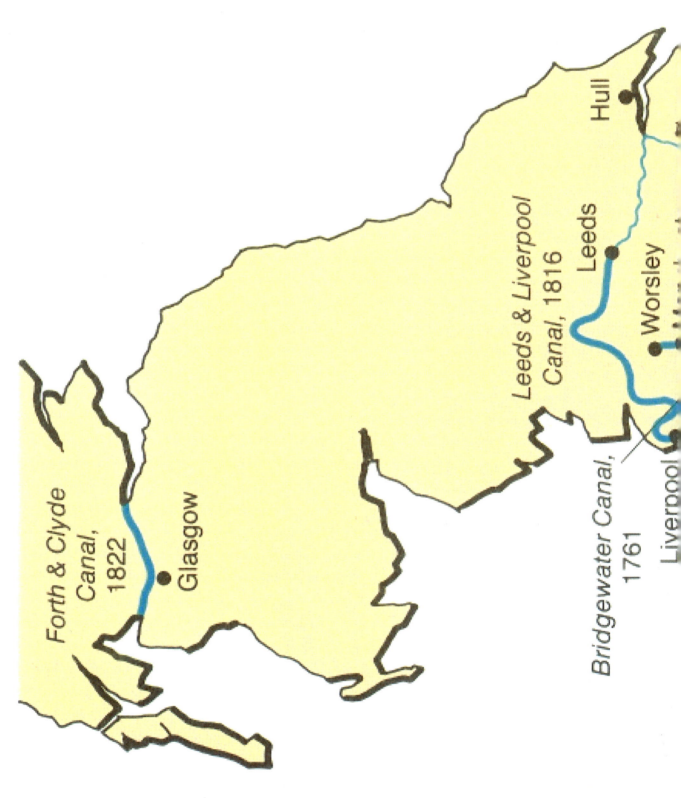

76 c. 2

Question

When was it possible to travel between the following places by canal and river?

In each case, write the names of the places and the route taken.

(a) Manchester to Liverpool

(b) Liverpool to Hull

(c) Birmingham to London

(d) Nottingham to London

(e) Bristol to London

(f) Glasgow to the North Sea

(g) Bristol to Hull

(h) Liverpool to Leeds

Ordinary people gained from the canals. Manufacturers and farmers had much lower costs, so they could reduce the price of their goods. Here are some examples.

76 c. 3

EFFECT OF CANALS ON COSTS OF TRANSPORT	BY ROAD	BY CANAL
Manchester to Birmingham (e.g. coal)	£4.0s.0d. per ton	£1.10s.0d. per ton
Stourport to Liverpool (e.g. finished pottery)	£5.0s.0d. per ton	£1.10s.0d. per ton

EFFECT OF CANALS ON PRICE OF COAL	BEFORE CANALS	AFTER CANALS
Coal prices in Manchester	11s.6d. per ton	5s.8d. per ton
Coal prices in Birmingham	15s.0d. per ton	4s.0d. per ton

The canals were also used for transporting passengers. On the Forth and Clyde canal 'fly boats' travelled 25 miles in three hours. This is very quick for a boat! Food and drink were provided, as well as entertainment in the form of newspapers and games.

We have seen some of the advantages of canals. But they also had some disadvantages. Some of these can be seen in these pictures:

A swift passenger boat, or 'fly boat'.

What do you think were the disadvantages of locks?

Canals could be dangerous!
Here a canal bank has burst.

77 c. 2

This complaint about canals was made to Parliament:

The canal companies have enjoyed a monopoly and they have abused their power. They have raised the price for carrying corn from 6s. 8d. a ton to 12s. 6d., and for cotton from 6s. 8d. to 15 shillings. The barges are poor, and have been wrecked in storms. The canal was closed for ten days in summer and frozen for weeks in winter. It sometimes took longer to get goods from Liverpool to Manchester than from New York to Liverpool.

Parliamentary Papers

No wonder some people were already looking for a better form of transport.

77 c. 3

Questions

1 Make up a poster or advertisement for
   canal transport
   Put in as much factual detail as you can.

2 From the pictures and the complaint
   made to Parliament, make a list of all the
   things that were wrong with canals.

15 The railways

Communications in Britain had improved a great deal in the 18th century. Passengers could travel by coach along the turnpikes far more quickly than ever before. Goods could be sent more cheaply and efficiently by sea and canal.

Little did the users of roads and canals realise how their opportunities for travel were soon to change even more dramatically! A few clever people were already thinking about a new and better form of transport. There was money to be made by anyone who came up with a workable idea. These people knew that:

(a) Rails made of stone or wood had been used for a long time for trucks in mines. Possibly tracks could be used to carry heavy goods over longer distances.

(b) Steam engines were used to power machinery. Possibly they could be made to turn the wheels of a locomotive.

(c) Better iron was being made, which meant that rails and engines could be made with greater strength and precision.

By putting these ideas together, some inventors came up with the first railway locomotives. These were first used in places such as mines. You can see one of them on trial in the picture following.

Trevithick's 'Catch me who can'.
What is happening in the picture?

These early locomotives were unreliable and dangerous, and were only used along short lines. Even so, some people believed that they could be improved and developed. One such person was George Stephenson. He has been called 'the father of the English railways', a name that reveals his eventual success, but he had many problems along the way.

Activity

Copy this flow diagram and complete it to show the factors that helped to make the first railway locomotives.

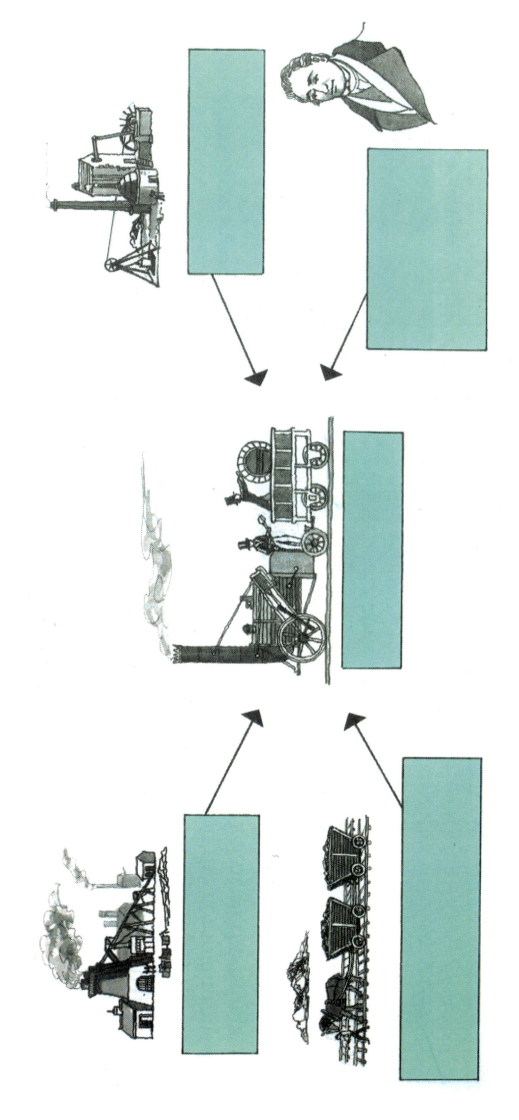

The opposition

Many people disliked the idea of railways. Here are some of the reasons why they opposed them:

A

Some people feared that there would be accidents: this one occurred near Clapham Junction, London, in 1868.

Railways could also cause inconvenience to others!

C

It was declared that the railway would prevent cows grazing and hens laying. The poisoned air from the locomotive would kill birds as they flew over them. Houses next to the line would be burnt up from the fire thrown from the engine chimneys. The air would be polluted by clouds of smoke. There would no longer be any use for horses, and there would be no use for oats and hay.

Questions

1   Make a list of all the arguments against railways given in sources **A-C**.

2   Study source **C** carefully. There are some clues here about the sort of people who feared railways the most. Who do you think these people might have been?

3   Can you think of a new idea today that is receiving the same sort of opposition? What is the idea, and what are the reasons against it? Do you agree with them?

The opening of the Stockton and Darlington railway.

Power for the railway

Many people liked the idea of railways, but they disagreed about what form of power should be used. In 1825 the first public railway opened, between Stockton and Darlington. Several forms of power were used on the line, as shown in this diagram.

80 c. 2

Darlington

Brussleton

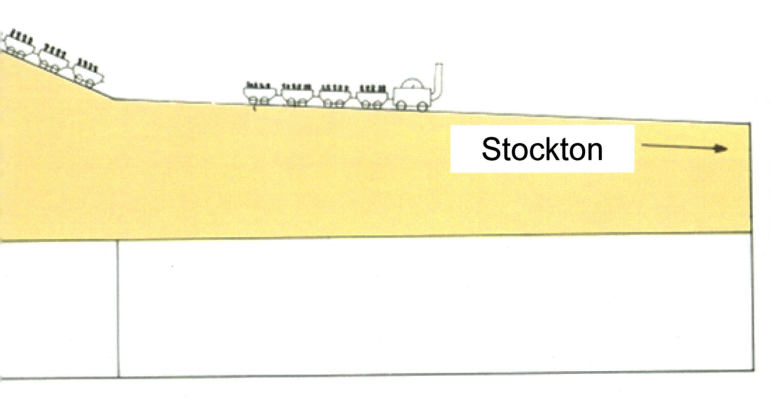

Activity

Copy and complete the diagram, writing in the appropriate places the forms of railway power used.

80 c. 4

The idea of a railway appealed to the merchants of Liverpool and Manchester. They employed Stephenson to build a new line. When he had finished, the directors decided to have a competition to see which form of power was best. In 1829 this advertisement appeared:

1829.

GRAND COMPETITION

OF

LOCOMOTIVES

ON THE

LIVERPOOL & MANCHESTER RAILWAY.

STIPULATIONS & CONDITIONS

ON WHICH THE DIRECTORS OF THE LIVERPOOL AND MANCHESTER RAILWAY OFFER A PREMIUM OF £500 FOR THE MOST IMPROVED LOCOMOTIVE ENGINE.

I.

The said Engine must "effectually consume its own smoke," according to the provisions of the Railway Act, 7th Geo. IV.

II.

The Engine, if it weighs Six Tons, must be capable of drawing after it, day by day, on a well-constructed Railway, on a level plane, a Train of Carriages of the gross weight of Twenty Tons, including the Tender and Water Tank, at the rate of Ten Miles per Hour, with a pressure of steam in the boiler not exceeding Fifty Pounds on the square inch.

III.

There must be Two Safety Valves, one of which must be completely out of the reach or control of the Engine-man, and neither of which must be fastened down while the Engine is working.

IV.

The Engine and Boiler must be supported on Springs, and rest on Six Wheels; and the height from the ground to the top of the Chimney must not exceed Fifteen Feet.

V.

The weight of the Machine, WITH ITS COMPLEMENT OF WATER in the Boiler, must, at most, not exceed Six Tons; and a Machine of less weight will be preferred if it draw AFTER it a PROPORTIONATE weight; and if the weight of the Engine, &c. do not exceed Five Tons, then the gross weight to be drawn need not exceed Fifteen Tons; and in that proportion for Machines of still smaller weight — provided that the Engine, &c., shall still be on six wheels, unless the weight (as above) be reduced to Four Tons and a Half or under, in which case the Boiler, &c., may be placed on four wheels. And the Company shall be at liberty to put the Boiler, Fire Tube, Cylinders, &c., to the test of a pressure of water not exceeding 150 Pounds per square inch, without being answerable for any damage the Machine may receive in consequence.

VI.

There must be a Mercurial Gauge affixed to the Machine, with Index Rod, showing the Steam Pressure above 45 Pounds per square inch; and constructed to blow out a Pressure of 60 Pounds per inch.

VII.

The Engine to be delivered complete for trial, at the Liverpool end of the Railway, not later than the 1st of October next.

VIII.

The price of the Engine which may be accepted, not to exceed £550, delivered on the Railway; and any Engine not approved to be taken back by the Owner.

N.B.—The Railway Company will provide the Engine Tender with a supply of Water and Fuel, for the experiment. The distance within the Rails is four feet eight inches and a half.

THE LOCOMOTIVE STEAM ENGINES,

WHICH COMPETED FOR THE PRIZE OF £500 OFFERED BY THE DIRECTORS OF THE LIVERPOOL AND MANCHESTER RAILWAY COMPANY.

DRAWN TO A SCALE ¼ INCH TO A FOOT.

THE "ROCKET" OF MR. ROBT. STEPHENSON OF NEWCASTLE,

THE "NOVELTY" OF MESSRS. BRAITHWAITE & ERRICSSON OF LONDON,

THE "SANSPAREIL" OF MR. HACKWORTH OF DARLINGTON,

page 81

Look at this table, which shows the outcome of the contest.

Engine	Appearance	Best performance	Overall performance
Novelty	Light copper and blue; looked nippy.	Reached 30 mph pulling 45 passengers, on 4th day of trial.	Three of the first five days were spent repairing the engine. On the sixth day the boiler collapsed.

| Sans Pareil | Green, yellow and black; looked heavy. | Reached 18 mph without a load. | The boiler failed on day 2. On day 5 the engine burned out. While working, the engine poured out hot cinders. Also, the engine broke the competition rules, being overweight. |
| Cycloped | A wagon was powered by a horse walking on a drive belt. | Reached 5 mph. | Disqualified. |

81 c. 2

Perseverance	Red wheels.	Reached 6 mph.	Was damaged on the way to the competition when a wagon overturned on the road. Five days were spent on repairs, and the engine was withdrawn after a short run.
Rocket	Yellow and black; white chimney.	Reached 30 mph unladen on over 20 runs. Hauled 12 ½ tons at 12 mph.	The Rocket was the only reliable engine. It could pull a heavy load and reach high speed. It was clearly the winner!

Not only did Stephenson win a prize, but he also got a contract to supply several more locomotives of the same type.

Activity

Use the evidence here to write a description of the Rainhill trials. This might take the form of a newspaper report. It should describe the atmosphere of the competition, the attitudes of the people there, the competition, and the results.

Building the lines

Building a railway is not easy. Before laying the rails a massive amount of preparation must be done. Railway builders knew that they had to make the lines as level as they could. To do this they needed to build embankments and dig cuttings and tunnels. To cross rivers they needed huge bridges. Remember that they did not have mechanical diggers as we do today. The work had to be done mainly by muscle power.

The men who provided this muscle power were called navvies. Some of them had been employed in digging canals or 'navigations' before the railways were begun. Railways were a far bigger job.

Look at these pictures and read the accounts of railway building.

82 c. 1

A A railway tunnel.

B
Excavation near Mount Olive, Liverpool.

82 c. 2

C Making the running.

D

'Making the running' was the most spectacular part of navvy work and one of the most dangerous. The runs were made by laying planks up the side of the cutting, up which barrows were wheeled. The running was made by the strongest of men. A rope, attached to the barrow and also to the man's belt, ran up the side of the cutting and round a pulley at the top. When the barrow was loaded a signal was given to the horse drawer at the top. The man was drawn up the side of the cutting, balancing the barrow in front of him. If on the upward climb the horse slipped or the man lost his balance on the muddy plank, then he had to do his best to save himself by throwing the loaded barrow to one side of the plank and himself to the other.

Coleman, 1965

83 c. 1

E

The tunnel, 30 feet high and 30 feet broad, was formed of bricks laid in cement. The bricklayers who were working on the roof were suddenly almost overwhelmed by a deluge of water which burst in upon there. The men were placed on a raft. In spite of every effort to keep it down, the water rose with such speed that the men were nearly jammed against the roof: The assistant engineer jumped overboard. Then, swimming with the rope in his mouth, he towed the raft to the foot of the nearest shaft through which he and his men were lifted up into daylight.

Head, 1849

Each of these problems - cuttings, tunnels, embankments and bridges - had to be tackled on the Liverpool-Manchester railway, as can be seen from the diagram following.

Activity

Write or tape a short discussion between two elderly navvies looking back on their greatest achievements and worst experiences. Put as much feeling into it as you can, but base it closely on the factual evidence presented above.

83 c. 3

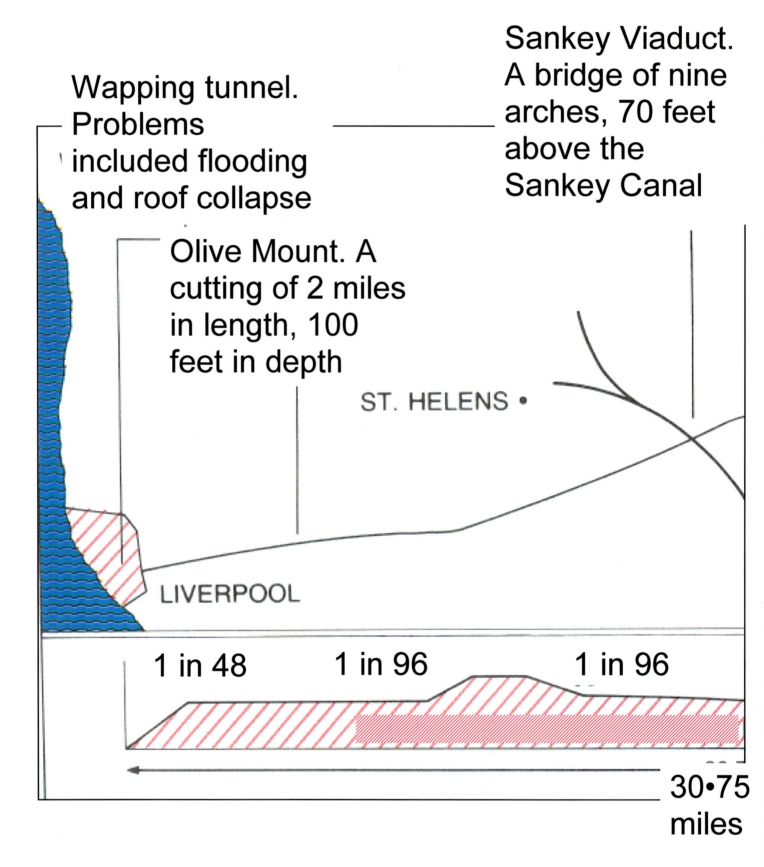

Chat Moss. A great bog of peat and quicksand. Having failed to create foundations, the embankment was built on a 'raft' of wood which 'floated' on the bog.

NEWTON

MANCHESTER

Sankey Canal

. WARRINGTON

Gradients between Liverpool and Manchester

Railway mania

You will have realised from the picture of the opening of the Stockton-Darlington railway and the Rainhill trials that railways amazed people who had never seen such things before.

Not everyone was impressed, though! Read these two accounts of travel on the Liverpool-Manchester line.

F

The experience of Fanny Kemble, an actress:

You cannot imagine how strange it seemed to be journeying on without any visible cause of progress other then the magical machine with its flying white breath. The engine was set off at its utmost speed, 35 miles an hour, swifter than a bird flies. The motion is as smooth as possible, too; I could have either read or written. When I closed my eyes the sensation was quite delightful. Yet strange as it was, I had not the slightest sense of fear.

G

The experience of Thomas Greevey, an MP:

Today I had the satisfaction, for I can't call it a pleasure, of taking a trip of five miles - and we did it in just a quarter of an hour - that is, twenty miles an hour. The quickest motion is to me frightful. It is like flying and it is impossible to get rid of the idea of death if the slightest accident happens. It gave me a bad headache. There is not much smoke, but there were sparks in the air. One burned Miss De Ross's cheek and another burned a hole in Lady Marian's silk dress. I am glad to have seen this miracle, and to have travelled in it, but this first journey will also be my last.

84 c. 2

Not many people shared Greevey's views. Nearly everyone wanted to travel on the railway. New railways were soon being built all over the country. Furthermore, the profits of the early railways were so high that many people wanted to buy shares in them. This was the first time that ordinary people invested in the stock market. This boom in railway shares was known as 'railway mania'. Many people made a lot of money, but some who invested in ill-considered schemes lost everything. Here are some cartoon views of railway mania.

Questions

1 Find as many points as you can where these two accounts agree.

2 Find as many points as you can where they disagree.

THE RAILWAY JUGGERNAUT OF 1845.

The 'break of gauge' at Gloucester: goods had to be transferred between trains.

One of the greatest problems of the early railways was the mixture of gauges. The two greatest railway builders, George Stephenson and I. K. Brunel, built lines of different widths.

85 c. 1

For practical reasons it was decided that the Stephenson gauge of 5' 81/2" should be the national gauge, and not Brunel's 7' 0". Even so, the Great Western Railway is still there to remind us of Brunel's work.

Isambard Kingdom Brunel.

85 c. 2

Questions

1. Why do you think that so many people bought railway shares?

2. Why, according to the cartoonists, were some of them mad to do so?

3. What do you think might be some of the 'practical reasons' why the narrower gauge was chosen?

Paddington Station, London: the terminus of the Great Western Railway.

The effects of railways

Study the following sources.

A

B

The Liverpool-Manchester railway.

E Travellers on the way to Epsom Races, 1847.

87 c. 1

F

The London and Greenwich railway.

87 c. 2

G

What a revolution in business when the ordinary rate of travelling shall be twenty miles instead of ten per hour. The traveller will live double times - by travelling in five hours where he used to require ten, he will have the other five at his disposal. The man of business in Manchester will breakfast at home, proceed to Liverpool by railway, transact his business, and return to Manchester before dinner.

Booth, 1830

87 c. 3

H

The Barentin viaduct on the Paris-Havre railway, France.

I

Telegraph wires ran alongside the railway.

THE WONDER of the AGE ! !

INSTANTANEOUS COMMUNICATION.

Under the special Patronage of Her Majesty & H.R.H. Prince Albert.

THE GALVANIC AND ELECTRO-MAGNETIC

TELEGRAPHS,

ON THE

GT. WESTERN RAILWAY.

May be seen in constant operation, daily, (Sundays excepted) from 9 till 8, at the

TELEGRAPH OFFICE, LONDON TERMINUS, PADDINGTON AND TELEGRAPH COTTAGE, SLOUGH STATION.

An Exhibition admitted by its numerous Visitors to be the most interesting and ATTRACTIVE of any in this great Metropolis. In the list of visitors are the illustrious names of several of the Crowned Heads of Europe, and nearly the whole of the Nobility of England.

"*This Exhibition, which has so much excited Public attention of late, is well worthy a visit from all who love to see the wonders of science.*"—MORNING POST.

The Electric Telegraph is unlimited in the nature and extent of its communications; by its extraordinary agency a person in London could converse with another at New York, or at any other place however distant, as easily and nearly as rapidly as if both parties were in the same room. Questions proposed by Visitors will be asked by means of this Apparatus, and answers thereto will instantaneously be returned by a person 20 Miles off, who will also, at their request, ring a bell or fire a cannon, in an incredibly short space of time, after the signal for his doing so has been given.

The Electric Fluid travels at the rate of 280,000 Miles per Second.

By its powerful agency Murderers have been apprehended, (as in the late case of Tawell,)—Thieves detected; and lastly, which is of no little importance, the timely assistance of Medical aid has been procured in cases which otherwise would have proved fatal.

The great national importance of this wonderful invention is so well known that any further allusion here to its merits would be superfluous.

N.B. Despatches sent to and fro with the most confiding secrecy. Messengers in constant attendance, so that communications received by Telegraph, would be forwarded, if required, to any part of London, Windsor, Eton, &c.

ADMISSION ONE SHILLING.

T. HOME, *Licensee.*

Norton, Printer, 48, Church St, Portman Market.

88 c. 1

J

5000 engines and 150 000 vehicles were run on the railways. Railway companies employed 90 400 officers and servants. The engines consumed annually 2 000 000 tons of coal. The wear and tear was great. 20 000 tons of iron were required annually, as well as 26 000 000 sleepers. . . .

Royal Statistical Society, 1866

Activity

Use all of these sources to describe the effects of the railways. You may wish to write under the following headings:

(a)   travel for business and leisure;

(b)   goods;

(c)   the economy (e.g. employment);

(d)   news;

(e)   town and countryside;

(f)   the losers.

Part F
Power and Poverty
17 People and power

In 1707, England and Wales were united with Scotland and became Great Britain. At this time Great Britain was ruled by the King or Queen, and Parliament. Today everyone has a say in government when he or she votes in an election. In the 18th century very few people had a vote, and Parliament was run by the upper classes.

These lords and gentlemen did what suited them. Acts of Parliament were generally for the benefit of the rich. They did very little to help the rest of the people. Usually the poor were left to fend for themselves.

King George III.

Gladstone addressing the House of Commons in 1833.

95 c. 2

Activity

Divide your page into two columns. In the left-hand column write the details of how Parliament worked before 1800. In the right-hand column write the equivalent for today.

1800	Today
Members of Parliament were from the upper class.	
Few people could vote.	
Qualifications for voting were different across the country.	
Some constituencies had fewer than ten voters.	
Elections were held every 7 years.	
At elections people declared in public who they were voting for.	
There were no real political parties.	
The King or Queen chose the Prime Minister.	

The election of Members of Parliament

Imagine an election with only a small number of voters, who have to shout out who they are voting for! Candidates would do anything to become Members of Parliament (MPs). No wonder 18th-century elections were often corrupt!

Study the following sources, and answer the questions that follow.

These paintings by Hogarth were criticisms of elections. One shows candidates trying to win votes; the other shows the day of voting.

96 c. 1

A

B

A letter from Philip Francis to Harriet Francis, 1802:

My own dear Harriet,

The fact is that yesterday morning I was unanimously elected by one elector to represent the Borough of Appleby in Parliament. There was no other candidate, no opposition, no vote. So I had nothing to do but thank the said elector for his unanimous vote. Then we had a great dinner at the castle, and a famous ball in the evening. On Friday morning I will leave this place with flying colours, and do not intend to see it again for another seven years.

96 c. 3

C

Old Sarum was once a large town. By 1800 only fields remained, but this 'Borough' still had two MPs. This contract, issued in 1749, shows how the purchase of land could also bring power:

His Royal Highness is willing to pay the sum of £3000 and a salary of £1500 a year on the condition that his Royal Highness shall have the nomination of each and every MP that shall be elected for the Borough of Old Sarum for __ years.

D

A letter from the Duke of Marlborough to the Duke of Newcastle, 1753:

My Dear Lord,

I hope you will excuse the present request but you know the need to trouble one's friends during an election. A poor woman in Oxford is under sentence of transportation for stealing a shift and an old cloak. It is her first offence, and I request that you pardon her. I am desired to beg the favour by several voters in Oxford, and can't at present well refuse. The woman's name is Ann Grant.

Your humble and obedient servant,

Marlborough.

page 97

Activity

Study sources **A-D** and find evidence to support each of these statements:

1   In some places there was no need for an election.

2   In some places very few people were entitled to vote.

3   Candidates had to spend a great deal of money to buy votes or bribe voters.

4   Candidates were willing to use all their influence to win votes.

5   Elections sometimes led to violence.

Reform and revolution

Many people demanded reform. They said that the vote should be given to many more people, and that any man - but not yet any woman! - should be able to become a Member of Parliament. In 1789, however, events took place in France which were to end any chance of reform - events which came to be known as the French Revolution.

In France also power was held by the King and the aristocracy. In Britain there was a huge gap between rich and poor, but in France the difference was even greater. In 1789 the poor could no longer stand this situation and took matters into their own hands. Under the slogan 'Liberty, equality and brotherhood' they plunged into revolution.

The Bastille was a prison in Paris. Its taking by the revolutionaries was a great blow against the government. Ever since, the incident has been a symbol of the revolution.

The execution of Louis XVI.

page 98

Read these accounts from British people who were caught up in the turmoil.

A

Early on Friday morning, the people took over the arsenal. Then they moved towards the palace with captured artillery. At 10 o'clock, the King saw that danger was near. He left the palace with the Royal Family and took shelter in the National Assembly building. A short time after this, fighting began between the people and the Swiss soldiers who were guarding the palace. The Swiss were overpowered and almost all killed; the number killed is still not known, but cannot have been less than 1500. An assembly declared that power was taken away from the King, that the people no longer trusted his ministers, and that a new government should be formed. It declared that a national convention would be held to decide the fate of the King and the way to make a new government. All citizens should be admitted without distinction of rank or station.

Lord Gower

98 c. 2

B

It was decided to execute the King. Here Henry Edgeworth, a priest who was in France at the time, describes what happened:

The procession lasted almost two hours; the streets were lined with citizens, all armed, some with pikes and some with guns.

The carriage was surrounded by a body of troops formed of the most desperate people in Paris. As another precaution, they had placed before the horses a number of drums, intended to drown any noise or murmur in favour of the King.

As soon as the King had left the carriage, three guards surrounded him, and would have taken off his clothes, but he repulsed them and undressed himself. They surrounded him again and would have seized his hands. 'What are you attempting?' said the King. 'To bind you', answered the wretches. 'No, I shall never consent to that.'

I saw him cross the scaffold with firm foot, and he pronounced these words:

'I die innocent of all the crimes laid to my charge. I pardon those who have caused my death. And I pray to God that the blood you are going to shed may never be visited on France.' He was going to say more but a man on horseback ordered the drums to beat. The executioners dragged him under the guillotine, which with one stroke severed his head from his body. A guard seized the head and showed it to the people. At first an awful silence prevailed; at length some cries of **'Vive la republique'** were heard.

98 c. 4

C

Many other executions followed. Any citizen could make an accusation against 'an enemy of the people'. Usually, citizens' courts condemned the accused to death. At the height of the Revolution even the leaders, such as Robespierre, were not safe. Here Archibald Rowan describes what he saw:

In two days after the execution of Robespierre the whole commune [a revolutionary group] of Paris, about sixty persons, were guillotined in less than an hour and a half. Although I was standing over a hundred paces from the place of execution, the blood of the victims streamed under my feet.

D

Here another witness, J. C. Mellingen, describes the guillotine:

> The process of execution was a sad and heart-rending spectacle. In the middle of the Place de la Revolution was a guillotine in front of a colossal statue of Liberty. On one side of the guillotine were drawn up a number of carts, with large baskets painted red to receive the heads and bodies of the victims. Most of the unfortunates ascended the scaffold with a determined step - many of them looked up firmly at the menacing instrument of death. When the neck was secured, the weighty knife was dropped with a heavy fall, and the executioners tossed the body into the basket, and threw the head in after it.
>
> **Thompson, 1938**

page 99

Questions

1 Use source A to describe how the King was overthrown.

2 What can you tell from source B about the sympathies of the witness? Explain your answer carefully, making detailed reference to the source.

3 If the writer of source B sympathises with one side, does that mean that the source has no value as historical evidence? Explain your answer carefully.

4 From the comments made in sources C and D, what do you think might have seemed most strange and awful to the British witnesses?

This cartoon sums up what many British people thought of the French Revolution

The British fleet, led by Admiral Nelson, defeated the French fleet at Trafalgar in 1805. Nelson was killed during the battle.

War with France

Although at first some British radicals, or reformers, had sympathy with the French people, they soon lost it. Most people in Britain were horrified by the events in France. There may well have been characters like the famous Scarlet Pimpernel who helped French aristocrats to escape '**Madame Guillotine**'.

France had become a revolutionary republic. The new government thought that it should help the people of other countries This cartoon sums up what many British people thought of the French Revolution to do the same. In 1793 French armies invaded the Netherlands. In 1796 they invaded Italy. Britain's government now decided that they must do something to stop the spread of revolution. So Britain went to war with France. The war lasted until 1815 when the French leader, Napoleon Bonaparte, was finally defeated at the battle of Waterloo. The French Revolution and the Napoleonic Wars had a great effect on politics in England. The government pointed to events in France as a warning of what could happen if they did not rule firmly. Instead of agreeing to reforms, the government dealt harshly with anyone who protested against them.

The British army, led by Wellington, defeated the French army at Waterloo in 1815.

100 c. 1

The Peterloo Massacre

The war had been good for Britain's economy and trade. Order books were full. People could find jobs and good wages. When the war ended there was a slump. For example, the textile industry had been benefiting from orders for uniforms and blankets. These orders stopped. Workers were dismissed and could not find other work. Also, prices were high and people could not afford to buy bread.

People had much to protest about. There were demonstrations by angry people up and down the country. One of the biggest demonstrations took place in 1819 at St. Peter's Fields in Manchester. The tragic events that followed are remembered as the 'Peterloo Massacre'.

Study the following sources and answer the questions that follow.

A

Henry Hunt was a main speaker at the demonstration. A few days before, he issued these instructions:

We will meet on Monday next, and by your steady, firm and sensible conduct will convince all your enemies that you have an important public duty to perform.

Our enemies will seek every opportunity to excite a riot, that they may have an excuse to spill our blood.

Come then to the meeting armed with no other weapon than your conscience.

100 c. 3

B

Samuel Bamford was another important speaker. In his memoirs he remembered what he said before the meeting:

I reminded them that they were going to attend the most important meeting that had ever been held for parliamentary reform. They were not to offer any insult or provocation by word or deed. If peace officers came to arrest myself or any other person, they were not to offer any resistance.

C

Archibald Prentice, a supporter of reform, remembered the demonstrators coming to the meeting:

> It seemed to be a gala day with the country people who were mostly dressed in their best and brought with them their wives and boys and girls.

D

Lieutenant Jolliffe of the 15th Hussars (a cavalry unit) was there with his troop. He also saw the crowd arriving:

> A solid mass of people moved along at brisk pace with five or six bands of music. Mr Hunt with two or three men and two women were in an open carriage drawn by the people.

101 c. 1

E

The historian Donald Read, writing in 1958, quoted estimates of the numbers at the meeting:

> The report in the **Manchester Observer** said that 153 000 people were present. The chairman of the committee of magistrates gave the total as 50-60 000.

F

Soon after the day of the demonstration, a government minister explained why an order for the arrest of the leaders was issued:

> The magistrates were convinced that the meeting bore the appearance of an insurrection [revolution] and would terrify the King's subjects, and nothing could justify it. Accordingly a warrant for the arrest of Hunt was drawn up.

Read, 1958

G

The yeomen, Manchester's part-time soldiers, were given the order to arrest Henry Hunt. The experienced hussars waited at the edge of the crowd in case of trouble. The Reverend Edward Stanley, an eyewitness, explained what happened next:

> The yeomen, inexperienced in such situations, rode into the crowd to arrest Hunt. As they approached, the dense mass of people used their utmost efforts to escape. But so closely were they pressed together that escape was impossible. On their arrival at the platform there was a scene of dreadful confusion. The speakers €ell or were forced off the stage.

101 c. 3

H

Another eyewitness remembers Henry Hunt's arrest:

> The magistrate said to Hunt, 'Sir, I have a warrant against you and arrest you as my prisoner.' Hunt replied, `I willingly surrender myself to any civil officer who will show me his warrant.'

I

Seeing that the militia were in difficulty, the hussars rode into the crowd to help them. Lieutenant Jolliffe remembers what happened:

> The hussars drove people forward with, the flats of their swords, but sometimes, as is almost inevitably the case, the edge was used.

J

The Reverend Edward Stanley saw what happened next:

The yeomanry were in difficulty, being crushed by the large crowd. The 15th Hussars pressed forward towards them. The people were now in a state o€ utter rout and confusion and hundreds were thrown down in the attempt to escape. During the confusion, made worse at the end by the rattle of artillery crossing the square, shrieks were heard in all directions. As the crowd dispersed the effect of the conflict became visible. Some were bleeding on the ground and unable to rise.

A cartoonist's version of events at 'Peterloo'.

K

This is an extract from the relief committee's report:

> Eleven people were killed or died from their injuries. 400 people were injured, 140 of these being the victims of sabre cuts.

L

Soon after, this article appeared in the Manchester Observer.

> The Prince Regent spoke of his great satisfaction at the prompt, decisive, and efficient measures taken for the preservation of public order by the authorities at St Peter's Fields.

102 c. 2

Questions

1 Study sources A, B, C and D.

What evidence is there to suggest that the demonstration would not be a threat to law and order?

Explain your answer carefully.

2 Study sources E and F.

Why do the authorities seem to have been so worried about the meeting?

3 Study G and H.

Why was it difficult for the magistrates to arrest Hunt?

4 Study G, I, J and K.

Explain how so many people came to be injured.

5 Why do you think that the Prince Regent sent the message quoted in source L?

6 How might the people quoted in this section have felt about the massacre at Peterloo?

7 What does the cartoon suggest about the attitude of the cartoonist towards the events at Peterloo?

102 c. 4

Slow change

Events like Peterloo worried the government so much that they passed strict laws making any protest meetings illegal. People could be arrested and imprisoned without trial. For those who were charged under these laws, the highest penalty was death.

At Lancaster eight persons were sentenced to death for rioting. All of them, man, woman and child, were executed. One of the victims was a boy so young that he called on his mother for help at the time of the execution, thinking she could save him.

Archibald Prentice, 1851

A cartoonist shows one view of freedom in Britain.

103 c. 1

Such punishments did not stop the protests. The government became convinced that it must allow some reform. If it did not do so there would be a revolution. However, it was not willing to give a vote to the working classes. Instead the government decided to get the middle class on its side. In the Reform Bill of 1832 the voting rights were extended to include the prosperous middle class. Before 1832, 500 000 people could vote. Now 800 000 could do so. This was still a small percentage of the population.

The Reform Bill also got rid of the 'Rotten Boroughs'. These were constituencies in which only a very few people were represented by a Member of Parliament. Instead, some growing industrial towns were allowed MPs of their own for the first time.

103 c. 2

The working people felt betrayed. They formed an organisation called the Chartist movement. It was given this name because it wanted Parliament to accept the demands of the people's charter. These were their demands:

103 c. 3

The Six Points

OF THE

PEOPLE'S

CHARTER.

1. A VOTE for every man twenty-one years of age, unless he is mad or a criminal.

2. A SECRET BALLOT, to allow every man to vote in secret without fear.

3. No PROPERTY QUALIFICATION to become a Member of Parliament - any man, rich or poor, can represent a constituency.

103 c. 4

4. PAYMENT OF MEMBERS OF PARLIAMENT, so that any person can afford to leave his work to serve his country.

5. EQUAL CONSTITUENCIES, so that each Member of Parliament represents the same number of people.

6. ANNUAL ELECTIONS to Parliament, to stop corruption in elections and to make sure that Members of Parliament do not defy or betray those who vote for them.

103 c. 5

Three times the charter was presented to Parliament, and three times it was thrown out. After the third defeat, in 1848, the Chartist movement collapsed. For the time being, government remained in the hands of the middle and upper classes.

Questions

1 Why do you think the government was so worried about the people getting a vote?

2 Which points of the people's charter have:
   (a)   been accepted as they stand?
   (b)   been improved upon?
   (c)   never happened?

18 The Great Exhibition

The Great Exhibition took place in 1851. The original idea was that the Exhibition should be a showplace for British industry, but it became much more than that. It was a celebration of Britain, the Empire, and the reign of Queen Victoria.

Joseph Paxton produced a design for the Exhibition building. It was to be built in Hyde Park, and made of glass. There was no need to cut down the trees in the park: they were left inside the building! The picture here gives an idea of the overall size. It covered 8 hectares of ground. The framework was of cast-iron girders and the main material was 93 000 square metres of glass. Inside, there were 13 kilometres of table space for the display of exhibits.

104 c. 1

The following pictures give some idea of the Exhibition and the impression it made on people of the time. Study the pictures carefully and then answer the questions on page 106.

104 c. 2

The opening ceremony.

Hardware.

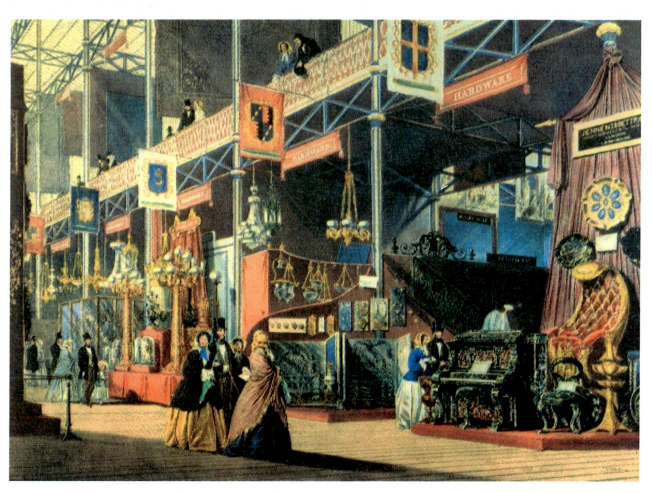

104 c. 3

Moving machinery.

India.

Canada.

page 106

Questions

Look carefully at all of the pictures.

1   Why do you think that the Exhibition building attracted so much attention?

2   What evidence is there in the pictures to show that the Exhibition was a showcase for British industry?

3   What evidence is there in the pictures to show that the Exhibition was a showcase for the Empire?

4   What evidence is there in the pictures and on page 86 to show what sort of people went to the Exhibition?

5 How might visitors have felt about Britain after a visit to the Exhibition? You could answer this question by discussing it in groups or by writing a conversation, for example.

Over 6 million visits were made to the Exhibition, more than 100 000 each day. People travelled by train from all over Britain. For many of them it was their first train journey, and the only visit they would ever make to the capital. People also came from all over the world.

106 c. 2

When the Exhibition had closed, the great palace of glass was dismantled and rebuilt - at Crystal Palace, in South London. Sadly, we have only pictures to show what it was like. Crystal Palace burned down in 1936. Despite this, there are other reminders of the Great Exhibition. £180 000 was made in profit. The money helped to provide the museums that you can still enjoy in Kensington, in London - the Science and Natural History Museums, and the Victoria and Albert Museum.

106 c. 3

The Victoria and Albert Museum, London.

106 c. 4

The Natural History Museum, London.

Vision Support Service
County Hall, Leicestershire

Produced under CLA Licence 2010

N24 Arial   April 2014

Questioning History is a complete series of evidence-based books for lower secondary level up to GCSE.

The course is accessible to students of all abilities, providing a motivating selection of sources, and building familiarity with historical skills and concepts through a variety of spoken and written responses.

Titles in the series
1 The Ancient World
2 The Middle Ages
3 The Early Modern Age
4 The Industrial Age
5 The Modern World

ISBN 0-17-435083-X